Accounting
Made Simple:

Accounting Explained
in 100 Pages or Less

Accounting Made Simple:

Accounting Explained in 100 Pages or Less

Mike Piper, CPA

Simple Subjects, LLC
ISBN: 978-0-9814542-2-1
www.ObliviousInvestor.com

Dedication

As always, for you, the reader.

Your Feedback is Appreciated.

As the author of this book, I'm very interested to hear your thoughts. If you find the book helpful, please let me know! Alternatively, if you have any suggestions of ways to make the book better, I'm eager to hear that too.

Finally, if you're unhappy with your purchase for any reason, let me know, and I'll be happy to provide you with a refund of the current list price of the book.

You can reach me at: mike@simplesubjects.com.

Best Regards,
Mike Piper

Table of Contents

Part Two
Generally Accepted
Accounting Principles (GAAP)

Introduction

Like the other books in the *"...in 100 Pages or Less"* series, this book is designed to give you a basic understanding of the topic (in this case, accounting), and do it as quickly as possible.

To be clear, the only way to pack a topic such as accounting into just 100 pages is to be as brief as possible. In other words, the goal is *not* to turn you into an expert. With 100 pages, it's simply not possible to provide a comprehensive discussion of every topic in the field of accounting.

That said, I *am* optimistic that this book will help you achieve a decent understanding of the most fundamental accounting concepts. (And, as explained more fully just before the table of contents, you're welcome to email me for a refund if you find yourself unsatisfied with the book.)

So What Exactly *Is* Accounting?

Some professors like to say that accounting is "the language of business." That definition has always been somewhat too abstract for my tastes. That said, all those professors are right.

At its most fundamental level, accounting is the system of tracking the income, expenses, assets, and debts of a business. When looked at with a trained eye, a business's accounting records truly tell the story of the business. Using nothing but a business's "books" (accounting records), you can learn practically anything about a business. You can learn simple things such as whether it's growing or declining, healthy or in trouble. Or, if you look closely, you can see things such as potential threats to the business's health that might not be apparent even to people within the company.

Where We're Going

This book is broken down into two main parts:

1. A discussion of the most important financial statements used in accounting: how to read each one, as well as what lessons you can draw from each.

2. A look at accounting using Generally Accepted Accounting Principles (GAAP), including:

    • Topics such as double entry bookkeeping, debits and credits, and the cash vs. accrual methods.

- How to account for some of the more complicated types of transactions, such as depreciation expense, gains or losses on sales of property, inventory and cost of goods sold, and so on.

So let's get started.

PART ONE

Financial Statements

CHAPTER ONE

The Accounting Equation

Before you can create financial statements, you need to first understand the single most fundamental concept of accounting: the accounting equation.

The accounting equation states that at all times, and without exceptions, the following will be true:

Assets = Liabilities + Owners' Equity

So what does that mean? Let's take a look at the equation piece by piece.

Assets: All of the property owned by the company.

Liabilities: All of the debts that the company currently has outstanding to lenders.

Owners' Equity (a.k.a. Shareholders' Equity): The company's ownership interest in its assets, after all debts have been repaid.

Let's use a simple, everyday example: homeownership.

EXAMPLE: Lisa owns a $300,000 home. To pay for the home, she took out a mortgage, on which she still owes $230,000. Lisa would be said to have $70,000 "equity in the home." Applying the accounting equation to Lisa's situation would give us this:

$$\text{Assets} = \text{Liabilities} + \text{Owners' Equity}$$
$$\$300,000 = \$230,000 + \$70,000$$

In other words, owners' equity (the part that often confuses people) is just a plug figure. It's simply the leftover amount after paying off the liabilities/debts. So while the accounting equation is conventionally written as:

Assets = Liabilities + Owners' Equity,

...it might be easier to think of it this way:

Assets − Liabilities = Owners' Equity

If, one year later, Lisa had paid off $15,000 of her mortgage, her accounting equation would now appear as follows:

$$\text{Assets} = \text{Liabilities} + \text{Owners' Equity}$$
$$\$300,000 = \$215,000 + \$85,000$$

Because her liabilities have gone down by $15,000—and her assets have not changed—her owner's equity has, by default, increased by $15,000.

My Asset is Your Liability

One concept that can trip up accounting novices is the idea that a liability for one person is, in fact, an asset for somebody else. For example, if you take out a loan with your bank, the loan is clearly a liability for you. From the perspective of your bank, however, the loan is an asset.

Similarly, the balance in your savings or checking account is, of course, an asset (to you). For the bank, however, the balance is a liability. It's money that they owe you, as you're allowed to demand full or partial payment of it at any time.

Chapter 1 Simple Summary[1]

- A company's assets consist of all the property that the company owns.

- A company's liabilities consist of all the debt that the company owes to lenders.

- A company's owners' equity is equal to the owners' interest in the company's assets, after paying back all the company's debts.

- The accounting equation is always written as follows:

  Assets = Liabilities + Owners' Equity

- However, it's likely easier to think of the accounting equation this way:

  Assets − Liabilities = Owners' Equity.

---

[1] Sample accounting problems for each chapter of this book are available at:
www.obliviousinvestor.com/example-accounting-problems
I suggest taking advantage of them if you feel that your understanding of a topic could use some help.

CHAPTER TWO

The Balance Sheet

A company's balance sheet shows its financial situation at a given point in time. It is, quite simply, a formal presentation of the accounting equation. As you'd expect, the three sections of a balance sheet are assets, liabilities, and owners' equity.

Have a look at the example of a basic balance sheet on the following page. Let's go over what each of the accounts refers to.

Assets

Cash and Cash Equivalents: Balances in checking and savings accounts, as well as any investments that will mature within 3 months or less.

Balance Sheet

Assets

Cash and Cash Equivalents	$50,000
Inventory	$110,000
Accounts Receivable	$20,000
Property, Plant, and Equipment	$300,000
Total Assets:	$480,000

Liabilities

Accounts Payable	$20,000
Notes Payable	$270,000
Total Liabilities:	$290,000

Owners' Equity

Common Stock	$50,000
Retained Earnings	$140,000
Total Owners' Equity	$190,000
Total Liabilities + Owners' Equity:	$480,000

Inventory: Goods kept in stock, available for sale.

Accounts Receivable: Amounts due from customers for goods or services that have already been delivered.

Property, Plant, and Equipment: Assets that cannot readily be converted into cash—things such as computers, manufacturing equipment, vehicles, furniture, etc.

Liabilities

Accounts Payable: Amounts due to suppliers for goods or services that have already been received.

Notes Payable: Contractual obligations due to lenders (e.g., bank loans).

Owners' Equity

Common Stock: Amounts invested by the owners of the company.

Retained Earnings: The sum of all net income over the life of the business that has not been distributed to owners in the form of a dividend. (If this is confusing at the moment, don't worry. It will be explained in more detail in Chapter 4, which discusses the statement of retained earnings.)

Current vs. Long-Term

Often, the assets and liabilities on a balance sheet will be broken down into current assets (or liabilities) and long-term assets (or liabilities). Current assets are those that are expected to be converted into cash within 12 months or less. Typical current assets include Accounts Receivable, Cash, and Inventory.

Everything that isn't a current asset is, by default, a long-term asset (a.k.a. non-current asset). For example, Property, Plant, and Equipment is a long-term asset account.

Current liabilities are those that will need to be paid off within 12 months or less. The most common example of a current liability is Accounts Payable. Notes Payable that are paid off over a period of time are split up on the balance sheet so that the next 12 months' payments are shown as a current liability, while the remainder of the note is shown as a long-term liability.

Multiple-Period Balance Sheets

What you'll often see when looking at published financial statements is a balance sheet—such as the one on the following page—that has two columns. One column shows the balances as of the end of the most recent accounting period, and the adjoining column shows the balances at the end of the prior period. This is done so that a reader can see how the financial position of the company has changed over time.

For example, looking at the balance sheet on the following page we can learn a few things about the health of the company. Overall, it appears that things are going well. The company's assets are increasing while its debt is being paid down.

The only thing that might be of concern is an increase in Accounts Receivable. An increase in Accounts Receivable could be indicative of trouble with getting clients to pay on time. On the other hand, it's also quite possible that it's simply the result of an increase in sales, and there's nothing to worry about.

Balance Sheet

Current Assets	12/31/13	12/31/12
Cash and Cash Equivalents	$50,000	$30,000
Accounts Receivable	$20,000	$5,000
Total Current Assets	$70,000	$35,000
Non-Current Assets		
Property, Plant, and Equipment	$330,000	$330,000
Total Non-Current Assets:	$330,000	$330,000
Total Assets	$400,000	$365,000
Current Liabilities		
Accounts Payable	$20,000	$22,000
Current Portion of Note Payable	$12,000	$12,000
Total Current Liabilities	$32,000	$34,000
Long-Term Liabilities		
Non-Current Portion of Note	$250,000	$262,000
Total Long-Term Liabilities	$250,000	$262,000
Total Liabilities:	$282,000	$296,000
Owners' Equity		
Common Stock	$30,000	$30,000
Retained Earnings	$88,000	$39,000
Total Owners' Equity	$118,000	$69,000
Total Liabilities + Equity:	$400,000	$365,000

Chapter 2 Simple Summary[1]

- A company's balance sheet shows its financial position at a given point in time. Balance sheets are formatted in accordance with the accounting equation:

  Assets = Liabilities + Owners' Equity

- Current assets are those that are expected to be converted into cash within 12 months or less. Any asset that is not a current asset is a non-current (a.k.a. long-term) asset by default.

- Current liabilities are those that will need to be paid off within the next 12 months. By default, any liability that is not a current liability is a long-term liability.

---

[1] Just a reminder: Sample accounting problems for each chapter of this book are available at:
www.obliviousinvestor.com/example-accounting-problems

CHAPTER THREE

The Income Statement

A company's income statement shows the company's financial performance over a period of time (usually one year). This is in contrast to the balance sheet, which shows financial position at a *point* in time. A frequently used analogy is that the balance sheet is like a photograph, while the income statement is more akin to a video.

The income statement—sometimes referred to as a profit and loss (or P&L) statement—is organized exactly how you'd expect. The first section details the company's revenues, while the second section details the company's expenses.

Income Statement	
Revenue	
Sales	$300,000
Cost of Goods Sold	(100,000)[1]
Gross Profit	200,000
Expenses	
Rent	30,000
Salaries and Wages	80,000
Advertising	15,000
Insurance	10,000
Total Expenses	135,000
Net Income	$65,000

Gross Profit and Cost of Goods Sold

Gross profit refers to the sum of a company's revenues, minus Cost of Goods Sold. Cost of Goods Sold (CoGS) is the amount that the company paid for the goods that it sold over the course of the period.

EXAMPLE: Laura runs a small business selling t-shirts with band logos on them. At the beginning of

---

[1] In accounting, negative numbers are indicated using parentheses.

the month, Laura ordered 100 t-shirts for $12 each. By the end of the month, she had sold all of the shirts for a total of $2,500. For the month, Laura's Cost of Goods Sold is $1,200, and her gross profit is $1,300.[1]

EXAMPLE: Rich runs a small business preparing tax returns. All of his costs are overhead—that is, each additional return he prepares adds nothing to his total costs—so he has no Cost of Goods Sold. His gross profit is simply equal to his revenues.

Operating Income vs. Net Income

Sometimes, you'll see an income statement—like the one on the following page—that separates operating revenues and expenses from non-operating revenues and expenses. Operating revenues are those coming from the sale of the business's primary products or services. Similarly, operating expenses are the expenses related to the core operation of the business. Things such as rent, insurance premiums, and employees' wages are typical operating expenses.

---

[1] If a company doesn't sell all of its inventory over the course of the period, the Cost of Goods Sold calculation becomes a little more involved. We'll be covering such calculations in Chapter 14.

Non-operating revenues and expenses are those that are unrelated to the core operations of the business and would include things such as interest income, interest expense, and gains or losses on investments.

Income Statement	
Revenue	
Sales	$450,000
Cost of Goods Sold	(75,000)
Gross Profit	375,000
Operating Expenses	
Rent	45,000
Salaries and Wages	120,000
Advertising	25,000
Insurance	10,000
Total Operating Expenses	200,000
Operating Income	175,000
Other Income and Expenses	
Gain on Sale of Investments	25,000
Interest Expense	(13,000)
Other Income, net	12,000
Net Income	$187,000

The point of separating operating revenues and expenses from non-operating revenues and expenses is to allow for the calculation of operating income. For some purposes, operating income is a more meaningful number than net income, because it provides a measure of how well the company is doing at its core business, without including the effects of financing and investment decisions.

Chapter 3 Simple Summary

- The income statement shows a company's financial performance over a period of time (usually a year).

- A company's gross profit is equal to its revenues minus its Cost of Goods Sold.

- A company's operating income is equal to its gross profit minus its operating expenses— the expenses that have to do with the core operation of the business.

- A company's net income is equal to all of its revenues and gains, minus all of its expenses and losses.

CHAPTER FOUR

The Statement of Retained Earnings

The statement of retained earnings is a very brief financial statement. (See example on following page.) It has only one purpose, which, as you would expect, is to detail the changes in a company's retained earnings over a period of time.

Again, retained earnings is the sum of all of a company's undistributed profits over the entire existence of the company. We say "undistributed" in order to distinguish from profits that *have* been distributed to company shareholders in the form of dividend payments.

EXAMPLE: ABC Construction is formed on January 1, 2013. At its date of formation, it naturally has a Retained Earnings balance of zero (because it hasn't had any net income yet).

Over the course of 2013, ABC Construction's net income is $50,000. In December of the year, it pays a dividend of $20,000 to its shareholders. Its retained earnings statement for the year would look as follows.

Statement of Retained Earnings	
Retained Earnings, 1/1/2013	$0
Net Income	50,000
Dividends Paid to Shareholders	(20,000)
Retained Earnings, 12/31/2013	$30,000

If, in 2014, ABC Construction's net income was $70,000 and it again paid a $20,000 dividend, its 2014 retained earnings statement would appear as follows:

Statement of Retained Earnings	
Retained Earnings, 1/1/2014	$30,000
Net Income	70,000
Dividends Paid to Shareholders	(20,000)
Retained Earnings, 12/31/2014	$80,000

Bridge Between Financial Statements

The statement of retained earnings functions much like a bridge between the income statement and the balance sheet. It takes information *from* the income statement, and it provides information *to* the balance sheet.

The final step of preparing an income statement is calculating the company's net income:

Income Statement	
Revenue	
Sales	$240,000
Gross Profit	240,000
Expenses	
Rent	70,000
Salaries and Wages	80,000
Total Expenses	150,000
Net Income	$90,000

Net income is then used in the statement of retained earnings to calculate the end-of-year balance in Retained Earnings:

Statement of Retained Earnings	
Retained Earnings, Beginning	$40,000
Net Income	90,000
Dividends Paid to Shareholders	(50,000)
Retained Earnings, Ending	$80,000

The ending Retained Earnings balance is then used to prepare the company's end-of-year balance sheet:

Balance Sheet	
Assets	
Cash and Cash Equivalents	$130,000
Inventory	80,000
Total Assets:	210,000
Liabilities	
Accounts Payable	20,000
Total Liabilities:	20,000
Owners' Equity	
Common Stock	110,000
Retained Earnings	80,000
Total Owners' Equity	190,000
Total Liabilities + Owners' Equity:	$210,000

Dividends: Not an Expense!

When first learning accounting, many people are tempted to classify dividend payments as an expense. It's true, they do look a lot like an expense in that they are a cash payment made from the company to another party.

Unlike many other cash payments, however, dividends are a *distribution* of profits (as opposed to expenses, which reduce profits). Because they are not a part of the calculation of net income, dividend payments do not show up on the income statement. Instead, they appear on the statement of retained earnings.

Retained Earnings: It's Not the Same as Cash

The definition of retained earnings—the sum of a company's undistributed profits over the entire existence of the company—makes it sound as if a company's Retained Earnings balance must be sitting around somewhere as cash in a checking or savings account. In all likelihood, however, that isn't the case at all.

Just because a company hasn't distributed its profits to its owners doesn't mean it hasn't already used them for something else. For instance, profits are frequently reinvested in growing the company by purchasing more inventory for sale or purchasing more equipment for production.

Chapter 4 Simple Summary

- The statement of retained earnings details the changes in a company's retained earnings over a period of time.

- The statement of retained earnings acts as a bridge between the income statement and the balance sheet. It takes information *from* the income statement, and it provides information *to* the balance sheet.

- Dividend payments are not an expense. They are a distribution of profits.

- Retained earnings is not the same as cash. Often, a significant portion of a company's retained earnings is spent on attempts to grow the company.

CHAPTER FIVE

The Cash Flow Statement

The cash flow statement does exactly what it sounds like: It reports a company's cash inflows and outflows over an accounting period.

Cash Flow Statement vs. Income Statement

At first, it may sound as if a cash flow statement fulfills the same purpose as an income statement. There are, however, some important differences between the two.

First, there are often differences in timing between when an income or expense item is recorded and when the cash actually comes in or goes out the door. We'll discuss this topic more thoroughly in Chapter 9: Cash vs. Accrual. For now, let's just consider a brief example.

EXAMPLE: In September, XYZ Consulting performs marketing services for a customer who does not pay until the beginning of October. In September, this sale would be recorded as an increase in both Sales and Accounts Receivable. (And the sale would show up on a September income statement.)

The cash, however, isn't actually received until October, so the activity would not appear on September's cash flow statement.

The second major difference between the income statement and the cash flow statement is that the cash flow statement includes several types of transactions that are not included in the income statement.

EXAMPLE: XYZ Consulting takes out a loan with its bank. The loan will not appear on the income statement, as the transaction is neither a revenue item nor an expense item. It is simply an increase of an asset (Cash) and a liability (Notes Payable). However, because it's a cash inflow, the loan *will* appear on the cash flow statement.

EXAMPLE: XYZ Consulting pays its shareholders a $30,000 dividend. As discussed in Chapter 4, dividends are not an expense. Therefore, the dividend will not appear on the income statement. It will, however, appear on the cash flow statement as a cash outflow.

Categories of Cash Flow

On a cash flow statement (such as the example later in this chapter) all cash inflows or outflows are separated into one of three categories:

1. Cash flow from operating activities,
2. Cash flow from investing activities, and
3. Cash flow from financing activities.

Cash Flow from Operating Activities

Technically, cash flow from operating activities includes any cash flows not specifically defined as investing or financing activities. The general idea, however, is to reflect most of the cash transactions that would be included in the determination of net income.

Common items that are categorized as cash flow from operating activities include:

- Receipts from the sale of goods or services,
- Payments made to suppliers,
- Payments made to employees,
- Interest payments made to lenders,
- Interest or dividends received from investments, and
- Tax payments.

Cash Flow from Investing Activities

Cash flow from investing activities includes cash spent on—or received from the sale of—investments in financial securities (stocks, bonds, etc.) as well as cash spent on—or received from the sale of—capital assets (i.e., assets expected to last longer than one year). Typical items in this category include:

- Purchase or sale of property, plant, or equipment, and
- Purchase or sale of stocks or bonds.

Cash Flow from Financing Activities

Cash flow from financing activities includes cash inflows and outflows relating to transactions with the company's owners and creditors. Common items that would fall in this category include:

- Cash received from investors when new shares of stock are issued,
- Dividends paid to shareholders,
- Cash received from taking out a loan, and
- Cash paid to pay back the *principal* on a loan. (Payments of interest are classified as an operating activity.)

Cash Flow Statement

Cash Flow from Operating Activities:

Cash receipts from customers	$320,000
Cash paid to suppliers	(50,000)
Cash paid to employees	(40,000)
Income taxes paid	(55,000)
Net Cash Flow From Operating Activities	175,000

Cash Flow from Investing Activities:

Cash spent on purchase of equipment	(210,000)
Net Cash Flow From Investing Activities	(210,000)

Cash Flow from Financing Activities:

Dividends paid to shareholders	(25,000)
Cash received from issuing new shares	250,000
Net Cash Flow From Financing Activities	225,000

Net increase in cash: $190,000

Chapter 5 Simple Summary

- The cash flow statement and the income statement differ in that they report transactions at different times. (We'll discuss this more thoroughly in Chapter 9: Cash vs. Accrual.)

- The cash flow statement also differs from the income statement in that it shows many transactions that would not appear on the income statement.

- Cash flow from operating activities includes most cash transactions that would factor into the calculation of net income.

- Cash flow from investing activities includes cash transactions relating to a company's investments in financial securities and cash transactions relating to long-term assets such as property, plant, and equipment.

- Cash flow from financing activities includes cash transactions between the company and its owners or creditors.

CHAPTER SIX

Financial Ratios

Of course, now that you know how to read financial statements, a logical next step would be to take a look at the different conclusions you can draw from a company's financials. For the most part, this work is done by calculating and comparing several different ratios.

Liquidity Ratios

Liquidity ratios are used to determine how easily a company will be able to meet its short-term financial obligations. Generally speaking, with liquidity ratios, higher is better. The most frequently used liquidity ratio is known as the current ratio:

$$\text{Current Ratio} = \frac{\text{Current Assets}}{\text{Current Liabilities}}$$

A company's current ratio provides an assessment of the company's ability to pay off its current liabilities (liabilities due within a year or less) using its current assets (cash and assets likely to be converted to cash within a year or less).

A company's quick ratio serves the same purpose as its current ratio: It seeks to assess the company's ability to pay off its current liabilities.

$$\text{Quick Ratio} = \frac{\text{Current Assets - Inventory}}{\text{Current Liabilities}}$$

The difference between quick ratio and current ratio is that the calculation of quick ratio excludes inventory balances. This is done in order to provide a worst-case-scenario assessment: How well will the company be able to fulfill its current liabilities if sales are slow (that is, if inventories are not converted to cash)?

EXAMPLE: ABC Toys (see balance sheet on the following page) would calculate its liquidity ratios as follows:

$$\text{Current Ratio} = \frac{40{,}000 + 100{,}000 + 60{,}000}{50{,}000 + 150{,}000} = 1$$

$$\text{Quick Ratio} = \frac{40{,}000 + 60{,}000}{50{,}000 + 150{,}000} = 0.5$$

A current ratio of 1 tells us that ABC Toys' current assets match its current liabilities, meaning it shouldn't have any trouble handling its financial obligations over the next 12 months.

However, a quick ratio of only 0.5 indicates that ABC Toys will need to maintain at least some level of sales in order to satisfy its liabilities.

Balance Sheet, ABC Toys	
Assets	
Cash and Cash Equivalents	$40,000
Inventory	100,000
Accounts Receivable	60,000
Property, Plant, and Equipment	300,000
Total Assets:	500,000
Liabilities	
Accounts Payable	50,000
Income Tax Payable	150,000
Total Liabilities:	200,000
Owners' Equity	
Common Stock	160,000
Retained Earnings	140,000
Total Owners' Equity	300,000
Total Liabilities + Owners' Equity:	$500,000

Profitability Ratios

While a company's net income is certainly a valuable piece of information, it doesn't tell the whole story in terms of how profitable a company really is. For example, Google's net income is going to absolutely dwarf the net income of your favorite local Italian restaurant. But the two businesses are of such different sizes that the comparison is rather mean-ingless, right? That's why we use the two following ratios:

$$\text{Return on Assets} = \frac{\text{Net Income}}{\text{Total Assets}}$$

$$\text{Return on Equity} = \frac{\text{Net Income}}{\text{Shareholders' Equity}}$$

A company's return on assets shows us the compa-ny's profitability in comparison to the company's size (as measured by total assets). In other words, return on assets seeks to answer the question, "How efficiently is this company using its assets to gener-ate profits?"

Return on equity is similar except that share-holders' equity is used in place of total assets. Return on equity asks, "How efficiently is this company using its investors' money to generate profits?"

By using return on assets or return on equity, you can actually make meaningful comparisons between the profitability of two companies, even if the companies are of very different sizes.

EXAMPLE: Using the previous balance sheet and the income statement below, we can calculate the following profitability ratios for ABC Toys:

$$\text{Return on Assets} = \frac{90,000}{500,000} = 18\%$$

$$\text{Return on Equity} = \frac{90,000}{300,000} = 30\%$$

Income Statement, ABC Toys	
Revenue	
Sales	$300,000
Cost of Goods Sold	(100,000)
Gross Profit	200,000
Expenses	
Rent	30,000
Salaries and Wages	80,000
Total Expenses	110,000
Net Income	$90,000

A company's gross profit margin shows what percentage of sales remains after covering the cost of the sold inventory. This gross profit is then used to cover overhead costs, with the remainder being the company's net income.

$$\text{Gross Profit Margin} = \frac{\text{Sales} - \text{Cost of Goods Sold}}{\text{Sales}}$$

EXAMPLE: Virginia runs a business selling cosmetics. Over the course of the year, her total sales were $80,000, and her Cost of Goods Sold was $20,000. Virginia's gross profit margin for the year is 75%, calculated as follows:

$$\frac{\text{Sales} - \text{Cost of Goods Sold}}{\text{Sales}} = \frac{\$80,000 - \$20,000}{\$80,000}$$

Gross profit margin is often used to make comparisons between companies within an industry. For example, comparing the gross profit margin of two different grocery stores can give you an idea of which one does a better job of keeping inventory costs down.

Gross profit margin comparisons across different industries can be rather meaningless. For instance, a grocery store is going to have a lower profit margin than a software company, regardless of which company is run in a more cost-effective manner.

Financial Leverage Ratios

Financial leverage ratios show the extent to which a company has used debt (as opposed to capital from investors) to finance its operations.

A company's debt ratio shows what portion of a company's assets has been financed with debt.

$$\text{Debt Ratio} = \frac{\text{Liabilities}}{\text{Assets}}$$

A company's debt-to-equity ratio shows the ratio of financing via debt to financing via capital from investors.

$$\text{Debt to Equity Ratio} = \frac{\text{Liabilities}}{\text{Owners' Equity}}$$

The Pros and Cons of Financial Leverage

It's obviously risky for a company to be very highly leveraged (that is, financed largely with debt). There is, however, something to be gained from using leverage. The more highly leveraged a company is, the greater its return on equity will be for a given amount of net income. That may sound confusing; let's look at an example.

EXAMPLE: XYZ Software has $200 million of assets, $100 million of liabilities, and $100 million of owners' equity. XYZ's net income for the year is $15 million, giving them a return on equity of 15% ($15 million net income divided by $100 million owners' equity).

If, however, XYZ Software's capital structure was more debt-dependent—such that they had $150 million of liabilities and only $50 million of equity—their return on equity would now be much greater. In fact, with the same net income, XYZ would have a return on equity of 30% ($15 million net income divided by $50 million owners' equity), thereby offering the company's owners twice as great a return on their money.

In other words, when the company's debt-to-equity ratio increased (from 1 in the first example to 3 in the second example), the company's return on equity increased as well, even though net income remained the same.

In short, the question of leverage is a question of balance. Being more highly leveraged (i.e., more debt, less investment from shareholders) allows for a greater return on the shareholders' investment. On the other hand, financing a company primarily with loans is obviously a risky way to run a business.

Asset Turnover Ratios

Asset turnover ratios seek to show how efficiently a company uses its assets. The two most commonly used turnover ratios are inventory turnover and accounts receivables turnover.

$$\text{Inventory Turnover} = \frac{\text{Cost of Goods Sold}}{\text{Average Inventory}}$$

The calculation of inventory turnover shows how many times a company's inventory is sold and replaced over the course of a period. The "average inventory" part of the equation is the average Inventory balance over the period, calculated as follows:

$$\text{Average Inventory} = \frac{\text{Beg. Inventory} + \text{Ending Inventory}}{2}$$

Inventory period shows how long, on average, inventory is on hand before it is sold.

$$\text{Inventory Period} = \frac{365}{\text{Inventory Turnover}}$$

A higher inventory turnover (and thus, a lower inventory period) shows that the company's inventory is selling quickly and is indicative that management is doing a good job of stocking products that are in demand.

41

A company's receivables turnover (calculated as credit sales over a period divided by average Accounts Receivable over the period) shows how quickly the company is collecting upon its Accounts Receivable.

$$\text{Receivables Turnover} = \frac{\text{Credit Sales}}{\text{Avg. Accounts Receivable}}$$

Average collection period is exactly what it sounds like: the average length of time that a receivable from a customer is outstanding prior to collection.

$$\text{Average Collection Period} = \frac{365}{\text{Receivables Turnover}}$$

Obviously, higher receivables turnover and lower average collection period is generally the goal. If a company's average collection period steadily increases from one year to the next, it could be an indication that the company needs to address its policies in terms of when and to whom it extends credit when making a sale.

Chapter 6 Simple Summary

- Liquidity ratios show how easily a company will be able to meet its short-term financial obligations. The two most frequently used liquidity ratios are current ratio and quick ratio.

- Profitability ratios seek to analyze how profitable a company is in relation to its size. Return on assets and return on equity are the most important profitability ratios.

- Financial leverage ratios express to what extent a company is using debt (instead of shareholder investment) to finance its operations.

- The more leveraged a company is, the higher return on equity it will be able to provide its shareholders. However, increasing debt financing can dramatically increase the business's risk level.

- Asset turnover ratios seek to show how efficiently a company uses its assets. Inventory turnover and receivables turnover are the most important turnover ratios.

PART TWO

Generally Accepted
Accounting Principles
(GAAP)

What is GAAP?

In the United States, Generally Accepted Accounting Principles (GAAP) is the name for the framework of accounting rules used in the preparation of financial statements. GAAP is created by the Financial Accounting Standards Board (FASB).

The goal of GAAP is to make it so that potential investors can compare financial statements of various companies in order to determine which one(s) they want to invest in, without having to worry that one company appears more profitable on paper simply because it is using a different set of accounting rules.

Who is Required to Follow GAAP?

All publicly traded companies are required by the Securities and Exchange Commission to follow

GAAP procedures when preparing their financial statements. In addition, because of GAAP's prevalence in the field of accounting, many companies follow GAAP even when they are not required to do so.

Governmental entities are required to follow GAAP as well. That said, there is a different set of GAAP guidelines (created by a different regulatory body) for government organizations. So, while they are following GAAP, their financial statements are quite different from those of public companies.

Chapter 7 Simple Summary

- Generally Accepted Accounting Principles (GAAP) is the framework of accounting rules and guidelines used in the preparation of financial statements.

- The Securities and Exchange Commission requires that all publicly traded companies adhere by GAAP when preparing their financial statements.

CHAPTER EIGHT

Debits and Credits

Most people (without knowing it) use a system of accounting known as single-entry accounting when they record transactions relating to their checking or savings accounts. For each transaction, one entry is made (either an increase or decrease in the balance of cash in the account).

Likely the single most important aspect of GAAP is the use of double-entry accounting, and the accompanying system of debits and credits. With double-entry accounting, each transaction results in two entries being made. (These two entries collectively make up what is known as a "journal entry.")

This is actually fairly intuitive when you think back to the accounting equation:

Assets = Liabilities + Owners' Equity.

If each transaction resulted in only one entry, the equation would no longer balance. That's why, with each transaction, entries will be recorded to two accounts.

EXAMPLE: A company uses $40,000 cash to purchase a new piece of equipment. In the journal entry to record this transaction, Cash will decrease by $40,000 and Equipment will increase by $40,000. As a result, the "Assets" side of the equation will have a net change of zero, and nothing changes at all on the "Liabilities + Owners' Equity" side of the equation.

Assets   = Liabilities + Owners' Equity
-40,000   no change   no change
+40,000

Alternatively, if the company had purchased the equipment with a loan, the journal entry would be an increase to Equipment of $40,000 and an increase to Notes Payable of $40,000. In this case, each side of the equation would have increased by $40,000.

Assets   = Liabilities + Owners' Equity
+40,000   +40,000   no change

So, What are Debits and Credits?

Debits and credits are simply the terms used for the two halves of each transaction. That is, each of these two-entry transactions involves a debit and a credit.

Now, if you've been using a bank account for any period of time, you likely have an idea that debit means decrease while credit means increase. That is, however, not exactly true. A debit (or credit) to an account may increase it or decrease it, depending upon what type of account it is:

- A debit entry will increase an asset account, and it will decrease a liability or owners' equity account.
- A credit entry will decrease an asset account, and it will increase a liability or owners' equity account.

From the perspective of your bank, your checking account is a liability—that is, it's money that they owe you. Because it's a liability, your bank credits the account to increase the balance and debits the account to decrease the balance.

Let's apply this system of debits and credits to our earlier example.

EXAMPLE: A company uses $40,000 cash to purchase a new piece of equipment. Cash will decrease by $40,000 and Equipment will increase by $40,000. To record this decrease to Cash (an asset account) we need to credit Cash for $40,000. To record this increase to Equipment (an asset account), we need to debit Equipment for $40,000.

This transaction could be recorded as a journal entry as follows:

DR. Equipment 40,000
    CR. Cash   40,000

As you can see, when recording a journal entry, the account that is debited is listed first, and the account that is credited is listed second, with an indentation to the right. Also, debit is conventionally abbreviated as "DR" and credit is abbreviated as "CR." (Often, these abbreviations are omitted, and credits are signified entirely by the fact that they are indented to the right.)

An easy way to keep everything straight is to think of "debit" as meaning "left," and "credit" as meaning "right." In other words, debits increase accounts on the left side of the accounting equation, and credits increase accounts on the right side. Also, this helps you to remember that the debit half of a journal entry is on the left, while the credit half is indented to the right.

Let's take a look at a few more example transactions and see how they would be recorded as journal entries.

EXAMPLE: Chris' Construction takes out a $50,000 loan with a local bank. Cash will increase by $50,000, and Notes Payable will increase by $50,000. To increase Cash (an asset account), we will debit it. To increase Notes Payable (a liability account), we will credit it.

DR. Cash   50,000
    CR. Notes Payable   50,000

EXAMPLE: Last month, Chris' Construction purchased $10,000 worth of building supplies, using credit to do so. Building Supplies (asset) and Accounts Payable (liability) each need to be increased by $10,000. To do so, we'll debit Building Supplies, and credit Accounts Payable.

DR. Building Supplies   10,000
    CR. Accounts Payable   10,000

Eventually, Chris's Construction will pay the vendor for the supplies. When they do, we'll need to decrease Accounts Payable and Cash by $10,000 each. To decrease a liability, we debit it, and to decrease an asset, we credit it.

DR. Accounts Payable   10,000
    CR. Cash   10,000

Revenue and Expense Accounts

So far, we've only discussed journal entries that deal exclusively with balance sheet accounts. Naturally, journal entries need to be made for income statement transactions as well.

For the most part, when making a journal entry to a revenue account, we use a credit, and when making an entry to an expense account, we use a debit. This makes sense when we consider that revenues increase owners' equity (and thus, like owners' equity, should be increased with a credit) and that expenses decrease owners' equity (and therefore, *unlike* owners' equity, should be increased with a debit).

EXAMPLE: Darla's Dresses writes a check for their monthly rent: $4,500. We need to decrease Cash and increase Rent Expense.

DR. Rent Expense   4,500
  CR. Cash   4,500

EXAMPLE: Connie, a software consultant, makes a sale for $10,000 and is paid in cash. We'll need to increase both Cash and Sales by $10,000 each.

DR. Cash   10,000
  CR. Sales   10,000

Sometimes a transaction will require two journal entries.

EXAMPLE: Darla's Dresses sells a wedding dress for $1,000 cash. Darla had originally purchased the dress from a supplier for $450. We have to increase Sales and Cash by $1,000 each. We also have to decrease inventory by $450 and increase Cost of Goods Sold (an expense account) by $450.

DR. Cash	1,000	
CR. Sales		1,000
DR. Cost of Goods Sold	450	
CR. Inventory		450

The General Ledger

The general ledger is the place where all of a company's journal entries get recorded. Of course, hardly anybody uses an actual paper document for a general ledger anymore. Instead, journal entries are entered into the company's accounting software, whether it's a high-end customized program, a more affordable program like QuickBooks, or even something as simple as a series of Excel spreadsheets.

The general ledger is a company's most important financial document, as it is from the general ledger's information that a company's financial statements are created.

T-Accounts

In many situations, it can be useful to look at all the activity that has occurred in a single account over a given time period. The tool most frequently used to provide this one-account view of activity is known as the "T-Account." One look at an example T-account and you'll know where it gets its name:

Cash	
400	200
550	950
300	

The above T-account shows us that, over the period in question, Cash has been debited for $400, $550, and $300, as well as credited for $200 and $950.

Often, a T-account will include the account's beginning and ending balances:

	Inventory	
Beginning Balance	600	200
	250	300
	500	
Ending Balance	850	

This T-account shows us that at the beginning of the period, Inventory had a debit balance of $600. It was then debited for a total of $750 (250+500) and credited for a total of $500 (200+300). As a result,

Inventory had a debit balance of $850 at the end of the period ($600 beginning balance, plus $250 net debit over the period).

The Trial Balance

A trial balance is simply a list indicating the balances of every single general ledger account at a given point in time. The trial balance is typically prepared at the end of a period, prior to preparing the primary financial statements.

The purpose of the trial balance is to check that debits—in total—are equal to the total amount of credits. If debits do not equal credits, you know that an erroneous journal entry must have been posted. While a trial balance is a helpful check, it's far from perfect, as there are numerous types of errors that a trial balance doesn't catch. (For example, a trial balance wouldn't alert you if the wrong asset account had been debited for a given transaction, as the error wouldn't throw off the *total* amount of debits.)

Chapter 8 Simple Summary

- For every transaction, a journal entry must be recorded that includes both a debit and a credit.

- Debits increase asset accounts and decrease equity and liability accounts.

- Credits decrease asset accounts and increase equity and liability accounts.

- Debits increase expense accounts, while credits increase revenue accounts.

- The general ledger is the document in which a company's journal entries are recorded.

- A T-account shows the activity in a particular account over a given period.

- A trial balance shows the balance in each account at a given point in time. The purpose of a trial balance is to check that total debits equal total credits.

CHAPTER NINE

Cash vs. Accrual

Individuals and most small businesses use a method of accounting known as "cash accounting." In order to be in accordance with GAAP, however, businesses must use a method known as "accrual accounting."

The Cash Method

Under the cash method of accounting, sales are recorded when cash is received, and expenses are recorded when cash is sent out. It's straightforward and intuitive. The problem with the cash method, however, is that it doesn't always reflect the economic reality of a situation.

EXAMPLE: Pam runs a retail ice cream store. Her lease requires her to prepay her rent for the next three months at the beginning of every quarter. For example, in April, she is required to pay her rent for April, May, and June.

If Pam uses the cash method of accounting, her net income in April will be substantially lower than her net income in May or June, even if her sales and other expenses are exactly the same from month to month. If a potential creditor was to look at her financial statements on a monthly basis, the lender would get the impression that Pam's profitability is subject to wild fluctuations. This is, of course, a distortion of the reality.

The Accrual Method

Under the accrual method of accounting, revenue is recorded as soon as services are provided or goods are delivered, regardless of when cash is received. (Note: This is why we use an Accounts Receivable account.)

Similarly, under the accrual method of accounting, expenses are recognized as soon as the company receives goods or services, regardless of when it actually pays for them. (Accounts Payable is used to record these as-yet-unpaid obligations.)

The goal of the accrual method is to fix the major shortcoming of the cash method: distortions of economic reality due to the frequent time lag between a service being performed and the service being paid for.

EXAMPLE: Mario runs an electronics store. On the 5th of every month, he pays his sales reps their commissions for sales made in the prior month. In August, his sales reps earned total commissions of $93,000. If Mario uses the accrual method of accounting, he must make the following entry at the end of August:

Commissions Expense	93,000	
Commissions Payable		93,000

Whenever an expense is recorded prior to its being paid for—such as in the above entry—the journal entry is referred to as an "accrual," hence, the "accrual method." The need for the above entry could be stated by saying that, at the end of August, "Mario has to accrue for $93,000 of Commissions Expense."

Then, on the 5th of September, when he pays his reps for August, he must make the following entry:

Commissions Payable	93,000	
Cash		93,000

A few points are worthy of specific mention. First, because Mario uses the accrual method, the expense is recorded when the services are performed, regardless of when they are paid for. This ensures that any financial statements for the month of August reflect the appropriate amount of Commissions Expense for sales made during the month.

Second, after both entries have been made, the net effect is a debit to the relevant expense account and a credit to Cash. (Note how this is exactly what you'd expect for an entry recording an expense.)

Last point of note: Commissions Payable will have no net change after both entries have been made. Its only purpose is to make sure that financial statements prepared at the end of August would reflect that—at that particular moment—an amount is owed to the sales reps.

Let's run through a few more examples so you can get the hang of it.

EXAMPLE: Lindsey is a freelance writer. During February she writes a series of ads for a local business and sends them a bill for the agreed-upon fee: $600. Lindsey makes the following journal entry:

Accounts Receivable	600	
Sales		600

When Lindsey receives payment, she will make the following entry:

Cash	600	
Accounts Receivable		600

EXAMPLE: On January 1st, when Lindsey started her business, she took out a 6-month, $15,000 loan with a local credit union. The terms of the loan were that, rather than making payments over the course of the loan, she would repay it all (along with $900 of interest) on July 1st.

Because Lindsey uses the accrual method, she must record the interest expense over the life of the loan, rather than recording it all at the end when she pays it off.

When Lindsey initially takes out the loan, she makes the following entry:

Cash	15,000	
Notes Payable		15,000

Then, at the end of every month, Lindsey records 1/6th of the total interest expense by making the following entry:

Interest Expense	150	
Interest Payable		150

On July 1st, Lindsey pays off the loan, making the following entry:

Notes Payable	15,000	
Interest Payable	900	
Cash		15,900

Prepaid Expenses

So far, all of our examples have looked at scenarios in which the cash exchange occurred *after* the goods/services were delivered. Naturally, there are occasions in which the opposite situation arises.

Again, the goal of the accrual method is to record the revenues or expenses in the period during which the real economic transaction occurs (as opposed to the period in which cash is exchanged). Let's revisit our earlier example of Pam with the ice cream store.

EXAMPLE: Pam's monthly rent is $1,500. However, Pam's landlord—Retail Rentals—requires that she prepay her rent for the next 3 months at the beginning of every quarter. On April 1st, Pam writes a check for $4,500 (rent for April, May, and June). She makes the following entry:

| Prepaid Rent | 4,500 | |
| Cash | | 4,500 |

In the above entry, Prepaid Rent is an asset account. Over the course of the three months, the $4,500 will be eliminated as the expense is recorded. Assets caused by the prepayment of an expense are known, understandably, as "prepaid expense accounts."

Then, at the end of each month (April, May, and June), Pam will make the following entry to record her rent expense for the period:

Rent Expense   1,500
        Prepaid Rent   1,500

Again, by the end of the three months, Prepaid Rent will be back to zero, and she will have recognized the proper amount of Rent Expense each month ($1,500). Of course, the process will start all over again on July 1st when Pam prepays her rent for the third quarter of the year.

Unearned Revenue

From Pam's perspective, the early rent payment created an asset account (Prepaid Rent). Naturally, from the perspective of her landlord, the early payment must have the opposite effect: It creates a liability balance known as "unearned revenue."

EXAMPLE: On April 1st, when Retail Rentals receives Pam's check for $4,500, they must set up an

Unearned Rent liability account. Then, they will record the revenue month by month.

On April 1st, Retail Rentals receives the check and makes the following entry:

Cash	4,500	
Unearned Rent		4,500

Then, at the end of each month, Retail Rentals will record the revenue by making the following entry:

Unearned Rent	1,500	
Rental Income		1,500

Chapter 9 Simple Summary

- In order to be in accordance with GAAP, businesses must use the accrual method of accounting (as opposed to the cash method).

- The goal of the accrual method is to recognize revenue (or expense) in the period in which the service is provided, regardless of when it is paid for.

CHAPTER TEN

The Accounting Close Process

As you know, the purpose of the Retained Earnings account is to show all of the net income that a business has earned over its life, excluding any income that has been distributed to shareholders. What we haven't yet discussed, however, is how any amounts actually *get into* the Retained Earnings account.

In addition, you know that the point of using revenue and expense accounts is to track the operations of a business over a period of time. But we have not yet discussed how, for example, *this* year's rent expense is separated from *last* year's rent expense, given that both are recorded in the same account.

The accounting close process is the answer to both of these questions.

Closing Journal Entries

At the end of each accounting period, all of the temporary accounts (i.e., revenue accounts, expense accounts, gain accounts, and loss accounts) are zeroed out, with an Income Summary account being used for the other half of the journal entry.

The purpose of zeroing out the balance in each of these accounts is to give them a fresh start for the next accounting period. That is, the idea is to ensure that, at any given time, a revenue account will show the amount of revenue that has been earned so far in that period, without including amounts from prior periods. (Ditto for expense accounts, gain accounts, and loss accounts.)

After all of the temporary accounts have been zeroed out, the Income Summary account will have a credit balance equal to the firm's net income for the period or a debit balance equal to the firm's net loss. This balance is then zeroed out and transferred to Retained Earnings.

EXAMPLE: Prior to the year-end close process, ABC Consulting's trial balance is as follows:

ABC Consulting Trial Balance 12/31/2013		
Account Title	**Debit**	**Credit**
Cash	70,000	
Accounts Receivable	30,000	
Investments	50,000	
Accounts Payable		10,000
Common Stock		40,000
Retained Earnings		45,000
Sales		200,000
Gain on Sale of Investments		10,000
Rent Expense	30,000	
Wages and Salary Expense	110,000	
Advertising Expense	15,000	
Total	305,000	305,000

To close out their books for the year, ABC's accountant will make the following journal entries[1]:

Sales	200,000	
Income Summary		200,000

Gain on Sale of Investments	10,000	
Income Summary		10,000

---

[1] Alternatively, these entries can be combined into one very large entry.

Income Summary	30,000	
Rent Expense		30,000
Income Summary	110,000	
Wages and Salary Expense		110,000
Income Summary	15,000	
Advertising Expense		15,000

After all of the temporary accounts have been closed, the Income Summary account will have a credit balance of $55,000, which represents the firm's $55,000 net income over the period. ABC's accountant would then make the following entry to close out the Income Summary account to Retained Earnings.[1]

Income Summary	55,000	
Retained Earnings		55,000

---

[1] The purpose of using an Income Summary account rather than closing out all of the income statement accounts directly to Retained Earnings is to keep the Retained Earnings account from getting cluttered with numerous journal entries at the end of each accounting period.

Chapter 10 Simple Summary

- At the end of each accounting period, closing journal entries are made to zero out the balance in revenue, expense, gain, and loss accounts—with an Income Summary account being used for the other half of each closing journal entry.

- After all the income statement accounts have been zeroed out, the Income Summary account will have a balance equal to the firm's net income or loss for the period. A journal entry is then made to transfer this balance into the Retained Earnings account.

CHAPTER ELEVEN

Other GAAP Concepts and Assumptions

Again, the goal of GAAP is to ensure that companies' financial statements are prepared using a consistent set of rules and assumptions so that they can be compared to those of another company in a meaningful way. In this chapter we'll examine a few of the assumptions that are used when preparing GAAP-compliant financial statements.

Historical Cost

Under GAAP, assets are generally recorded at their historical cost (i.e., the amount paid for them). This seems obvious, but there are times in which it would appear reasonable for a company to report an asset at a value other than the amount paid for it. For example, if a company has owned a piece of real estate for several decades, reporting the piece of land at its historical cost may very significantly under-state the value of the land.

However, if GAAP allowed companies to use any other valuation method—current market value for instance—it would introduce a great deal of subjectivity into the process. (To use the example of real estate again: Depending upon what method you use or who you ask, you could find several different answers for the fair market value of a piece of real estate.) Instead, GAAP usually requires that companies report assets using the most objective value: the cost paid for them.

Materiality

Under GAAP, the materiality (or immateriality) of a transaction refers to the impact that the transaction will have on the company's financial statements. If an omission of a given transaction could cause a viewer of the company's financial statements to make a different decision than he or she would make if the transaction were reported correctly, the trans-action is said to be "material."

EXAMPLE: Martin's business currently has $50,000 of current assets, $20,000 of current liabilities, and owes $75,000 on a loan that will be due in 2 years. The loan is clearly material, as an exclusion of the amount from the company's balance sheet would very likely lead a potential investor (or creditor) to make a poor decision regarding investing in (or lending money to) the company.

EXAMPLE: Carly runs a graphic design business. Her monthly revenues are usually around $20,000, and her monthly expenses are approximately $8,000. In August, Carly purchases $80 worth of office supplies, but she forgets to record the purchase.

While Carly should certainly make sure to record the purchase once she notices her error, the $80 expense is clearly immaterial. If creditors were looking at her financial statements at the end of August, the $80 understatement of expenses would be unlikely to cause them to make a different decision than they would make if the expense had been accurately recorded.

Monetary Unit Assumption

GAAP makes the assumption that the dollar is a stable measure of value. It's no secret that this is a faulty assumption due to inflation constantly changing the real value of the dollar. The reason for using such a flawed assumption is that the benefit gained from adjusting the value of assets on a regular basis to reflect inflation would be far outweighed by the cost in both time and money of requiring companies to do so.

Entity Assumption

For GAAP purposes, it's assumed that a company is an entirely separate entity from its owners. This concept is known as the "entity assumption" or "entity concept."

One important ramification of the entity assumption is the requirement for documenting transactions between a company and its owners. For example, if you wholly own a business, any transfers from the business's bank account to your bank account need to be recorded, despite the fact that it doesn't exactly seem like a "transaction" in that you're really just moving around your own money.

Matching Principle

According to GAAP, the matching principle dictates that expenses must be matched to the revenues that they help generate, and they must be recorded in the same period in which the revenues are recorded. This concept goes hand-in-hand with the concept of accrual accounting. For example, it's the matching principle that dictates that a company's utility expenses for the month of March must be recorded in March (rather than in April, when they are likely paid). The reasoning is that March's utility expenses contribute to the production of March's revenues, so they must be recorded in March.

Similarly, it is the matching principle that dictates that if a company purchases an asset that is expected to provide benefit to the company for multiple accounting periods (a desk, for instance), the cost of the asset must be spread out over the period for which it is expected to provide benefits. This process is known as depreciation, and we'll discuss it more thoroughly in Chapter 12.

Chapter 11 Simple Summary

- An asset's historical cost is often quite different from its current market value. However, due to its objective nature, historical cost is generally used when reporting the value of assets under GAAP.

- A transaction is said to be immaterial if an omission of the transaction would not result in a significant misstatement of the company's financial statements.

- Under GAAP, in order to simplify accounting, currency is generally assumed to have a stable value. This is known as the monetary unit assumption.

- For GAAP accounting, a business is considered to be an entirely separate entity from its owners. This is known as the entity concept or entity assumption.

- According to GAAP's matching principle, expenses must be reported in the same period as the revenues which they help produce.

CHAPTER TWELVE

Depreciation of Fixed Assets

As mentioned briefly in the previous chapter, when a company buys an asset that will probably last for greater than one year, the cost of that asset is not counted as an immediate expense. Rather, the cost is spread out over several years through a process known as depreciation.

Straight-Line Depreciation

The most basic form of depreciation is known as straight-line depreciation. Using this method, the cost of the asset is spread out evenly over the expected life of the asset.

EXAMPLE: Daniel spends $5,000 on a new piece of equipment for his carpentry business. He expects the equipment to last for 5 years, by which point it will likely be of no substantial value. Each year, $1,000 of the equipment's cost will be counted as an expense.

When Daniel first purchases the equipment, he would make the following journal entry:

Equipment   5,000
    Cash   5,000

Then, each year, Daniel would make the following entry to record Depreciation Expense for the equipment:

Depreciation Expense   1,000
    Accumulated Depreciation   1,000

Accumulated Depreciation is what's known as a "contra account," or more specifically, a "contra-asset account." Contra accounts are used to offset other accounts. In this case, Accumulated Depreciation is used to offset Equipment.

At any given point, the net of the debit balance in Equipment, and the credit balance in Accumulated Depreciation gives us the net Equipment balance—sometimes referred to as "net book value." In the example above, after the first year of depreciation expense, we would say that Equipment has a net book value of $4,000. ($5,000 original cost, minus $1,000 Accumulated Depreciation.)

We make the credit entries to Accumulated Depreciation rather than directly to Equipment so that we:

1. Have a record of how much the asset originally cost, and
2. Have a record of how much depreciation has been charged against the asset already.

EXAMPLE (CONTINUED): Eventually, after 5 years, Accumulated Depreciation will have a credit balance of $5,000 (the original cost of the asset), and the asset will have a net book value of zero. When Daniel disposes of the asset, he will make the following entry:

Accumulated Depreciation	5,000	
Equipment		5,000

After making this entry, there will no longer be any balance in Equipment or Accumulated Depreciation.

Salvage Value

What if a business plans to use an asset for a few years, and then sell it before it becomes entirely worthless? In these cases, we use what is called "salvage value." Salvage value (sometimes referred to as residual value) is the value that the asset is expected to have after the planned number of years of use.

EXAMPLE: Lydia spends $11,000 on office furniture, which she plans to use for the next ten years, after which she believes it will have a value of approximately $2,000. The furniture's original cost, minus its expected salvage value is known as its depreciable cost—in this case, $9,000.

Each year, Lydia will record $900 of depreciation as follows:

Depreciation Expense	900	
Accumulated Depreciation		900

After ten years, Accumulated Depreciation will have a $9,000 credit balance. If, at that point, Lydia does in fact sell the furniture for $2,000, she'll need to record the inflow of cash, and write off the Office Furniture and Accumulated Depreciation balances:

Cash	2,000	
Accumulated Depreciation	9,000	
Office Furniture		11,000

Gain or Loss on Sale

Of course, it's pretty unlikely that somebody can predict *exactly* what an asset's salvage value will be several years from the date she bought the asset. When an asset is sold, if the amount of cash received is greater than the asset's net book value, a gain must be recorded on the sale. (Gains work like revenue in that they have credit balances and increase owners' equity.) If, however, the asset is sold for less than its net book value, a loss must be recorded. (Losses work like expenses: They have debit balances, and they decrease owners' equity.)

Determining whether to make a gain entry or a loss entry is never too difficult: Just figure out whether an additional debit or credit is needed to make the journal entry balance.

EXAMPLE (CONTINUED): If, after ten years, Lydia had sold the furniture for $3,000 rather than $2,000, she would record the transaction as follows:

Cash	3,000	
Accumulated Depreciation	9,000	
Office Furniture		11,000
Gain on Sale of Furniture		1,000

EXAMPLE (CONTINUED): If, however, Lydia had sold the furniture for only $500, she would make the following entry:

Cash	500	
Accumulated Depreciation	9,000	
Loss on Sale of Furniture	1,500	
Office Furniture		11,000

Other Depreciation Methods

In addition to straight-line, there are a handful of other (more complicated) methods of depreciation that are also GAAP-approved. For example, the double declining balance method consists of multiplying the remaining net book value by a given percentage every year. The percentage used is equal to double the percentage that would be used in the first year of straight-line depreciation.

EXAMPLE: Randy purchases $10,000 of equipment, which he plans to depreciate over five years. Using straight-line, Randy would be depreciating 20% of the value (100% ÷ five years) in the first year. Therefore, the double declining balance method will use 40% depreciation every year (2 x 20%). The depreciation for each of the first four years would be as follows:

Year	Net Book Value			Depreciation Expense
1	$10,000	x 40%	=	$4,000
2	$6,000	x 40%	=	$2,400
3	$3,600	x 40%	=	$1,440
4	$2,160	x 40%	=	$864

EXAMPLE (CONTINUED): Because the equipment is being depreciated over five years, Randy would record $1,296 (that is, 2,160 – 864) of depreciation expense in the fifth year in order to reduce the asset's net book value to zero.

Another GAAP-accepted method of depreciation is the units of production method. Under the units of production method, the rate at which an asset is depreciated is not a function of time, but rather a function of how much the asset is used.

EXAMPLE: Bruce runs a business making leather jackets. He spends $50,000 on a piece of equipment that is expected to last through the production of 5,000 jackets. Using the units of production method of depreciation, Bruce would depreciate the equipment each period based upon how many jackets were produced (at a rate of $10 depreciation per jacket).

If, in a given month, Bruce's business used the equipment to produce 150 jackets, the following entry would be used to record depreciation:

Depreciation Expense   1,500
    Accumulated Depreciation   1,500

Immaterial Asset Purchases

The concept of materiality plays a big role in how some assets are accounted for. For example, consider the case of a $15 wastebasket. Given the fact that a wastebasket is almost certain to last for greater than one year, it should, theoretically, be depreciated over its expected useful life.

However, in terms of the impact on the company's financial statements, the difference between depreciating the wastebasket and expensing the entire cost right away is clearly negligible. The benefit of the additional accounting accuracy is far outweighed by the hassle involved in making insignificant depreciation journal entries year after year. As a result, assets of this nature are generally expensed immediately upon purchase rather than depreciated over multiple years. Such a purchase would ordinarily be recorded as follows:

Office Administrative Expense   15.00
    Cash (or Accounts Payable)   15.00

Chapter 12 Simple Summary

- Straight-line depreciation is the simplest depreciation method. Using straight-line, an asset's cost is depreciated over its expected useful life, with an equal amount of depreciation being recorded each month.

- Accumulated depreciation—a contra-asset account—is used to keep track of how much depreciation has been recorded against an asset so far.

- An asset's net book value is equal to its original cost, less the amount of accumulated depreciation that has been recorded against the asset.

- If an asset is sold for *more* than its net book value, a gain must be recorded. If it's sold for *less* than net book value, a loss is recorded.

- Immaterial asset purchases tend to be expensed immediately rather than being depreciated.

Amortization of Intangible Assets

Intangible assets are real, identifiable assets that are not physical objects. Common intangible assets include patents, copyrights, and trademarks.

Amortization

Amortization is the process—very analogous to depreciation—in which an intangible asset's cost is spread out over the asset's life. Generally, intangible assets are amortized using the straight-line method over the shorter of:

- The asset's expected useful life, or
- The asset's legal life.

EXAMPLE: Kurt runs a business making components for wireless routers. In 2013, he spends $60,000 obtaining a patent for a new method of production that he has recently developed. The patent will expire in 2033.

Even though the patent's legal life is 20 years, its useful life is likely to be much shorter, as it's a near certainty that this method will become obsolete in well under 20 years, given the rapid rate of innovation in the technology industry. As such, Kurt will amortize the patent over what he projects to be its useful life: four years. Each year, the following entry will be made:

Amortization Expense	15,000	
Accumulated Amortization		15,000

Chapter 13 Simple Summary

- Amortization is the process in which an intangible asset's cost is spread out over the asset's life.

- The time period used for amortizing an intangible asset is generally the shorter of the asset's legal life or expected useful life.

CHAPTER FOURTEEN

Inventory and Cost of Goods Sold

Under GAAP, there are two primary methods of keeping track of inventory: the perpetual method and the periodic method.

Perpetual Method of Inventory

Any business that keeps real-time information on inventory levels and that tracks inventory on an item-by-item basis is using the perpetual method. For example, retail locations that use barcodes and point-of-sale scanners are utilizing the perpetual inventory method.

There are two main advantages to using the perpetual inventory system. First, it allows a business to see exactly how much inventory they have on hand at any given moment, thereby making it easier to know when to order more. Second, it improves the accuracy of the company's financial statements because it allows very accurate recordkeeping as to the Cost of Goods Sold over a given period. (CoGS will simply be calculated as the sum of the costs of all of the particular items sold over the period.)

The primary disadvantage to using the perpetual method is the cost of implementation.

Periodic Method of Inventory

The periodic method of inventory is a system in which inventory is counted at regular intervals (at month-end, for instance). Using this method, a business will know how much inventory it has at the beginning and end of every period, but it won't know precisely how much inventory is on hand in the middle of an accounting period.

A second drawback of the periodic method is that the business won't be able to track inventory on an item-by-item basis, thereby requiring assumptions to be made as to which particular items of inventory were sold. (More on these assumptions later.)

Calculating CoGS under the Periodic Method of Inventory

When using the periodic method, Cost of Goods Sold is calculated using the following equation:

$$\text{Beginning Inventory} + \text{Inventory Purchases} - \text{Ending Inventory} = \text{Cost of Goods Sold}$$

This equation makes perfect sense when you look at it piece by piece. Beginning inventory, plus the amount of inventory purchased over the period gives you the total amount of inventory that *could* have been sold (sometimes known, understandably, as Cost of Goods Available for Sale). We then assume that, if an item isn't in inventory at the end of the period, it must have been sold. (And conversely, if an item *is* in ending inventory, it obviously wasn't sold, hence the subtraction of the ending inventory balance when calculating CoGS).

EXAMPLE: Corina has a business selling books on eBay. An inventory count at the beginning of November shows that she has $800 worth of inventory on hand. Over the month, she purchases another $2,400 worth of books. Her inventory count at the end of November shows that she has $600 of inventory on hand.

Using the equation above, we learn that Corina's Cost of Goods Sold for November is $2,600, calculated as follows:

Beginning Inventory	+ Purchases	-	Ending Inventory	=	Cost of Goods Sold
800	+ 2,400	-	600	=	2,600

Granted, this equation isn't perfect. For instance, it doesn't keep track of the cost of inventory theft. Any stolen items will accidentally get bundled up into CoGS, because:

1. They aren't in inventory at the end of the period, and
2. There is no way to know which items were stolen as opposed to sold, because inventory isn't being tracked item-by-item.

Assumptions Used in Calculating CoGS under the Periodic Method

Of course, the calculation of CoGS is a bit more complex out in the real world. For example, if a business is dealing with changing per-unit inventory costs, assumptions have to be made as to which ones were sold (the cheaper units or the more expensive units).

EXAMPLE: Maggie has a business selling t-shirts online. She gets all of her inventory from a single vendor. In the middle of April, the vendor raises its prices from $3 per shirt to $3.50 per shirt. If Maggie sells 100 shirts during April—and she has no way of knowing which of those shirts were purchased at which price—should her CoGS be $300, $350, or somewhere in between?

The answer depends upon which inventory-valuation method is used. The three most-used methods are known as FIFO, LIFO, and Average Cost. Under GAAP, a business can use any of the three.

First-In, First-Out (FIFO)

Under the "First-In, First-Out" method of calculating CoGS, we assume that the oldest units of inventory are always sold first. So in the above example, we'd assume that Maggie sold all of her $3 shirts before selling any of her $3.50 shirts.

Last-In, First-Out (LIFO)

Under the "Last-In, First-Out" method, the opposite assumption is made. That is, we assume that all of the newest inventory is sold before any older units of inventory are sold. So, in the above example, we'd assume that Maggie sold all of her $3.50 shirts before selling any of her $3 shirts.

EXAMPLE (CONTINUED): At the beginning of April, Maggie's inventory consisted of 50 shirts—all of which had been purchased at $3 per shirt. Over the month, she purchased 100 shirts, 60 at $3 per shirt, and 40 at $3.50 per shirt. In total, Maggie's Goods Available for Sale for April consists of 110 shirts at $3 per shirt, and 40 shirts at $3.50 per shirt.

 If Maggie were to use the **FIFO** method of calculating her CoGS for the 100 shirts she sold in April, her CoGS would be $300. (She had 110 shirts that cost $3, and FIFO assumes that all of the older units are sold before any newer units are sold.)

$$100 \times 3 = 300$$

If Maggie were to use the **LIFO** method of calculating her CoGS for the 100 shirts she sold in April, her CoGS would be $320. (LIFO assumes that all 40 of the newer, $3.50 shirts would have been sold, and the other 60 must have been $3 shirts.)

$$(40 \times 3.5) + (60 \times 3) = 320$$

It's important to note that the two methods result not only in different Cost of Goods Sold for the period, but in different ending inventory balances as well.

Under FIFO—because we assumed that all 100 of the sold shirts were the older, $3, shirts—it would be assumed that, at the end of April, her 50 remaining shirts would be made up of 10 shirts that were purchased at $3 each, and 40 that were purchased at $3.50 each. Grand total ending inventory balance: $170.

In contrast, the LIFO method would assume that—because all of the newer shirts were sold—the remaining shirts must be the older, $3 shirts. As such, Maggie's ending inventory balance under LIFO is $150.

Average Cost

The average cost method is just what it sounds like. It uses the beginning inventory balance and the purchases over the period to determine an average cost per unit. That average cost per unit is then used to determine both the CoGS and the ending inventory balance.

$$\frac{\text{Beg. Inventory} + \text{Purchases (in dollars)}}{\text{Beg. Inventory} + \text{Purchases (in units)}} = \text{Average Cost per Unit}$$

Avg. Cost per Unit x Units Sold = Cost of Goods Sold

Avg. Cost/Unit x Units in End. Inv. = End. Inv. Balance

EXAMPLE (CONTINUED): Under the average cost method, Maggie's average cost per shirt for April is calculated as follows:

Beginning Inventory: 50 shirts ($3 per shirt)
Purchases: 100 shirts (60 at $3 per shirt and 40 at $3.50 per shirt)

Her total units available for sale over the period is 150 shirts. Her total Cost of Goods Available for Sale is $470 (110 shirts at $3 each and 40 at $3.50 each).

Maggie's average cost per shirt = $470/150 = $3.13

Using an average cost per shirt of $3.13, we can calculate the following:

CoGS in April = $313 (100 shirts x $3.13 per shirt)

Ending Inventory = $157 (50 shirts x $3.13 per shirt)

Chapter 14 Simple Summary

- The perpetual method of inventory involves tracking each individual item of inventory on a minute-to-minute basis. It can be expensive to implement, but it improves and simplifies accounting.

- The periodic method of inventory involves doing an inventory count at the end of each period, then mathematically calculating Cost of Goods Sold.

- FIFO (first-in, first-out) is the assumption that the oldest units of inventory are sold before the newer units.

- LIFO (last-in, first-out) is the opposite assumption: The newest units of inventory are sold before older units are sold.

- The average cost method is a formula for calculating CoGS and ending inventory based upon the average cost per unit of inventory available for sale over a given period.

CONCLUSION

The Humble Little Journal Entry

The goal of accounting is to provide people— both internal users (managers, owners) and external users (creditors, investors)—with information about a company's finances. This information is provided in the form of financial statements. These financial statements are compiled using information found in the general ledger, which is, essentially, the collection of all of a business's journal entries.

In this way, we can see that it's the humble little journal entry (and its respective components: debits and credits) that provides the information upon which decisions are made in the world of business. Tens of billions of dollars change hands every day based ultimately upon the journal entries recorded by accountants—and accounting software— around the world.

These journal entries are based, in turn, upon the framework provided by the accounting equation and the double-entry accounting system that goes along with it.

Meanwhile, it's the guidelines provided by GAAP that make these journal entries (and the financial statements they eventually make up) meaningful. Because without the consistency of accounting provided for by GAAP, making a worthwhile comparison between two companies' financial statements would prove impossible.

APPENDIX

Helpful Online Resources

www.ObliviousInvestor.com
> The author's blog. Includes a wide variety of articles regarding personal finance, accounting, and taxation.

www.quickbooks.com
> Run by Intuit, this program is an excellent bookkeeping resource.

www.fasb.org
> The website of the Financial Accounting Standards Board, the organization responsible for creating and updating GAAP.

Also by Mike Piper

Can I Retire? Managing Your Retirement Savings Explained in 100 Pages or Less

Independent Contractor, Sole Proprietor, and LLC Taxes Explained in 100 Pages or Less

Investing Made Simple: Investing in Index Funds Explained in 100 Pages or Less

LLC vs. S-Corp vs. C-Corp Explained in 100 Pages or Less

Oblivious Investing: Building Wealth by Ignoring the Noise

Social Security Made Simple: Social Security Retirement Benefits Explained in 100 Pages or Less

Taxes Made Simple: Income Taxes Explained in 100 Pages or Less

INDEX

U